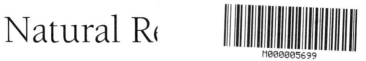

Natural R(

by Colin Kong

What are resources?

Everything we need comes from natural resources. A **natural resource** is any useful material that comes from Earth. Natural resources are important because living things need them.

When trees are cut down, the logs are shipped to lumber or paper mills.

Some resources can be replaced. Trees that grow in soil are a good example. People cut down trees for wood. Wood is used to build new houses. Wood chips can be turned into pulp to make paper.

When trees are cut down, we can plant new ones to replace them. After a short time these new trees will be tall enough to cut down. A resource that can be replaced is called a **renewable resource.**

Lumber mills cut the logs into boards. The boards are used to build new houses.

Resources That Cannot Be Replaced

Many natural resources are hidden deep underground. Miners have to dig up rocks called ores. Ores contain metals or minerals that people use.

Steel is made from iron. Many things are made of steel, such as forks and buses. There is a limited amount of iron ore underground. It cannot be replaced. A **nonrenewable resource** is a resource that cannot be replaced.

Hematite is an ore that contains the metal iron. Iron is used to make steel.

Using Resources	
Resource	**Uses**
Oil	Gasoline, paint, plastic, shampoo
Coal	Electricity, heat, paint thinner, insecticides
Iron ore	Machines, bicycles, autos, buildings

Coal, oil, and natural gas are also nonrenewable resources. They are fuels that release energy when burned. When we use up the natural resources in one area, we need to find new places to dig for them.

An Endless Supply of Resources

Some natural resources will never be used up. We have an ongoing supply of sunlight, air, and water. These resources are always available on Earth.

Mining can permanently change the Earth's surface. This open-pit mine is an example.

How can we protect our resources?

Using Resources Responsibly

People can save fuel in different ways. They can walk, ride a bicycle, or take a bus. When people buy products with less packaging, they are saving paper and plastic. These are ways to conserve. **Conservation** is using natural resources in a way that does not waste them or use them up.

Here, dirty water is piped into a wetland. Once it is cleaned naturally by a wetland, it will flow back into a river. Then the water can be used again.

Clean water is a resource we can conserve by using less of it. For example, when you are brushing your teeth, you can turn the water off.

To conserve water, many communities clean used water. To do this, they pipe dirty water into a wetland. Soil in the wetland pulls out harmful particles. Next, plants and tiny living things destroy the particles. Then, the cleaned water flows back into a river. Now, people can use it again.

These ponds of sand filter and clean harmful particles from dirty water. Then, farmers can use the recycled water.

Soil must be used wisely too. Some farmers plant crops around hills. If the crops were planted up and down the hills, water could wash away the soil. Farmers also plant trees around their fields to keep soil from blowing away.

Cities are growing. So people build on farmland. The soil is then lost to farming. How can we protect farmland for future generations?

We could allow these leaves to decay. They would turn into compost. Compost can add nutrients to soil.

Using Up Land Space for Trash

We throw away things we no longer need. Then a truck moves our trash to a landfill. Trash is buried in landfills. The trash never really goes away. Landfills are filling up quickly.

We can reduce the space we need for landfills. One way is to burn garbage in special furnaces. But then smoke from the burning must be cleaned. It can harm the air we breathe. We can also make less trash.

More than 200 million tons of trash is put into landfills in the United States each year.

What are ways to use resources again?

Using Resources Again

You conserve resources when you reuse things. Cloth napkins and empty jars can be reused. You can also give away your old clothes for others to use.

These are everyday objects. Can you think of some ways to use these materials again?

Another way to conserve resources is by recycling. When you **recycle** something, it is changed so that it can be used again. Useful resources can be made into new products. We use recycled metal, glass, plastic, and paper all the time.

This bench is made of recycled plastic.

Glass is often recycled. At the recycling plant, glass is sorted by color. Next, it is broken into pieces called shards. They are shipped to glass companies.

1 Sort glass.

2 Ship to glass company.

At the glass companies, the shards pass under a magnet to remove metal caps and rings. Shards are crushed into small particles called cullet. Cullet is cleaned, dried, and melted in furnaces. This glass can now be made into bottles, jars, or windowpanes. Recycled glass can be used over and over.

4 Make new glass bottles.

3 Process crushed glass.

Using Recycled Materials

Reusing and recycling are not new. Your great-grandparents may have bought flour in cloth sacks. Then they may have reused the cloth for rags, towels, or clothes. People have been recycling for years.

Today, it is easy to recycle. Many towns collect items to be recycled. Movie theaters and office buildings have special containers for bottles and cans. Grocery stores collect used shopping bags to be recycled.

This wall was made by reusing materials such as old tires and aluminum cans.

Conservation includes using products made from recycled materials. Sleeping bags you buy can have stuffing made out of shredded plastic bottles. Or you can buy a sweater with yarn recycled from old clothing.

The Three *R's*

There is an easy way to remember how to protect our natural resources. Remember the three *R's*— reduce, reuse, and recycle.

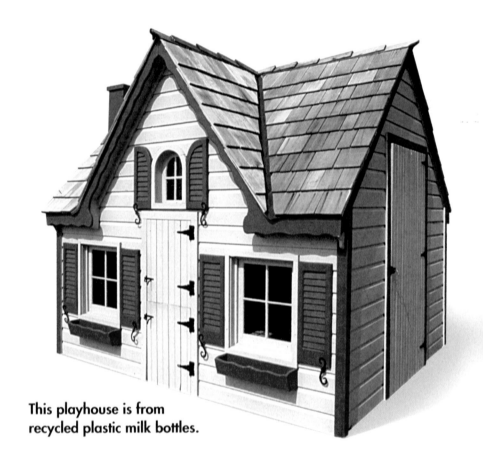

This playhouse is from recycled plastic milk bottles.

Glossary

conservation use of natural resources in a way that does not waste them or use them up

natural resource an important material from Earth that living things need

nonrenewable resource a resource that cannot be replaced after it is used up

recycle to change something so that it can be used again

renewable resource a resource that can be replaced in a fairly short time

What did you learn?

1. What are three examples of nonrenewable resources?

2. How can farmers conserve soil?

3. Why is it easy to recycle today?

4. **Writing** in Science In this book, you read about landfills and the need to reduce, reuse, and recycle our resources. Write to explain how reducing, reusing, and recycling would affect our landfills. Use examples from the book to support your answer.

5. **Compare and Contrast** How are renewable resources similar to nonrenewable resources? How are they different?

Genre	Comprehension Skill	Text Features	Science Content
Nonfiction	Compare and Contrast	• Captions • Labels • Call outs • Glossary	Natural Resources

Scott Foresman Science 3.9

PEARSON
Scott Foresman

scottforesman.com

ISBN 0-328-13832-0

90000

9 780328 138326

HEART, MIND, AND STRENGTH

THEORY AND PRACTICE FOR CONGREGATIONAL LEADERSHIP

JEFFREY D. JONES

FOREWORD BY PETER J. GOMES